# Journalling School

## A Short Course in Personal Journalling

by Ray Blake

# Introduction

The 15th of February 2005 was an important day for me. It was the day I began the journal that I have maintained almost every day since.

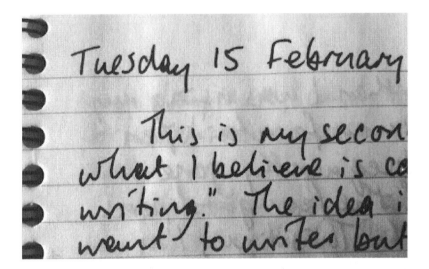

In the last decade and more, I have learned an awful lot about journalling. Indeed, I have learned a lot about writing generally. When I began I was very unsure about how to start, what to write about, how much to write - both in terms of the volume of text and its content - but I've slowly worked most of it out over the years.

So I thought I'd pass on some of the things that I've learned in a series of articles that I'm going to call 'Journalling School'. I hope that it will be useful for three kinds of people:

- People who have never thought of journalling before but who might like to give it a try
- People who have tired journalling in the past but abandoned it, who would perhaps like a kick start to get going again
- People who are already writing journals but would like some new ideas to inspire their day-to-day entries

It's called 'Journalling School' but you don't need to enroll. There are no exams or registers and you cannot possibly fail.

I'd love to hear from people about their journalling experiences and ideas; I'm convinced we learn best when we share.

# Session 1: Recording your life

*Welcome to the first session of Journalling School. Today's session is about why you might want to keep a written record of your life and how to get started.*

Life for most of us happens very quickly. Often we do not have time to assimilate events and experiences, but simply allow ourselves to be carried from one episode to the next. Holidays and special times pass in an instant. But a month, even a week after they are finished, how much of their detail is forgotten?

Keeping a journal is something most of us will have tried once or twice when we were younger. For many people, a childhood journal is the start of a record they continue to keep throughout adulthood, but for others interest wanes fairly quickly, perhaps before the first full week passes. So why should you add to your already full schedule by making time to keep a journal? Well, some of the benefits you might derive are listed below.

1. You create a permanent log of certain events, such as when you had a particular business idea, when

your child lost his first tooth, or how much you paid for that antique chair. When you start writing, you won't know how useful this might be in the future, but it will be.

2. By writing, you get to filter events and feelings and your brain gets a chance to process them properly, a chance that otherwise it rarely gets. Without this opportunity, it is difficult to fully appreciate what is going on in your life and what it means.

3. You are able over time to check progress towards a goal or other long-term changes in your life. When trying out a new personal development idea, for instance, you can log your progress and reactions as you go and later look back to see the long term change.

4. Your handwriting quality and/or speed will improve if you use a pen; your keyboard skills will improve if you use a PC.

5. Writing can help you solve problems in your life. The act of writing is slower than the act of thinking, so you have to slow down and be more careful in your approach. Opportunities and ideas you would otherwise have missed can flow in this environment.

Writing your journal isn't really about following rules, and absolutely any subject is fair game. You can write about the events of the day or the week and your reaction to them. You can use it to consider choices you are facing, sound off on something that angers you, or brainstorm ideas for meeting your goals. Or write about plans, dreams, fears or chicken livers. It's up to you. I tend when I'm journalling to try and write grammatically in paragraphs, because this helps me order my thoughts better, but if you want to cast syntax aside and write a stream of consciousness that's fine too. The only real rule is: write about what matters to you.

People sometimes find it difficult to start a journal, and there is a certain amount of self-consciousness involved that you will need to get past. The best advice is probably to trick yourself into it. Decide that you're not actually going to write about yourself, but simply record some random thoughts and ideas, perhaps with a view to improving your writing, trying out a new pen, or keyboard, or word processor.

Maintain this 'random writing' for a few days and without ever trying or meaning to you will simply start writing about what is happening to you or around you and how you feel about it. And then you're off.

## Homework

If you haven't started a journal yet, find a comfortable place where you'll have a little time for yourself, and start. Write the date and under that write about anything you like; it doesn't have to be about you. Write until you feel like stopping. Then stop. If you like, do this more than once.

If you are already writing a journal, then one day this week make your entry about how and why you began your journal. Write about what were you were hoping to achieve in journalling and reflect on how well that has panned out. Think and write about the unexpected benefits and rewards you've got from it.

*That was the first session of Journalling School. In the next session we'll look at sustaining the habit.*

# Session 2: Sustainable journalling

*Welcome to the second session of Journalling School. Today's session is about how to keep going.*

Often, it can be hard to sustain writing in a journal. Perhaps you get suddenly busy and lose any possibility of spare time, or perhaps it seems that nothing interesting is going on. Maybe you just forget to write a few days in a row and then the momentum is lost. There are ways to guard against this:

1.  Try to develop the habit of writing at the same time every day, say first thing in the morning, or last thing at night. One reader, Josh, says he writes just before bed and this helps him to 'close the day'. If you're working, could you devote a few minutes to this in your lunch break?

2.  Don't beat yourself up about making an entry every day; if circumstances mean just one or two entries a week, that's fine. You can increase or decrease the frequency of entries as you like.

3.  Unless your PC is always with you and ready to go, use pen and paper, and keep them with you all the time if you can so you can snatch writing

opportunities as they arise. Notebook users will find this very natural.

4. Use a plain paper notebook rather than a pre-printed diary, because you might want to write a lot some days, a little on others and sometimes nothing at all. Often, using a pre-printed journal, having a fixed space for each day can feel like tyranny. Conversely, for some people it may represent a good discipline.

5. If you get stuck with nothing to write, just write yourself a question, take a breath and write down some answers to it. I've included some prompt questions to get you started at the end of this post.

6. Think what it would be like if you had started a year ago. Imagine all the detail you would be able to go back and read.

7. If you do lapse for a period, don't consider the whole thing a failure. When you're ready, simply turn to a new page, write the date and start going again.

Look forward to the time when you will be able to look back and find out what you were doing and how you were feeling a year ago or ten years ago. What memories you are preserving for your future, or for your children?

# Journal prompt questions

When you're stuck, just write down any of these questions and then answer it. This can be the starting point for quite a long journal entry.

- How am I feeling right now and why?
- What was the best thing that happened today?
- What is worrying me?
- How will I spend the coming weekend?
- What ambition have I had for a long time?
- Who are the people that matter to me and why?
- What is my earliest memory?
- Where have I travelled and what did I see or do there?
- If I could do anything with my life, what would I do?
- If I won or inherited a fortune, what would I do with it?
- What values do I want my children to hold?
- How will I celebrate my next major birthday?
- What would my ideal holiday be like?

## Staying positive

You'll notice that among the prompts above, there are plenty of upbeat, positive topics. These give you a chance to break away from current concerns for a while. Now and then, this is important, because if your journal becomes a place in which you just whine and wallow, your motivation to keep writing will suffer, and so will your mood.

In a future session, I'll be talking about using journalling to influence your mood and to effect change, but for now make sure you choose strongly positive topics to journal about now and then.

## Homework

If you haven't started a journal after last week's session, try to start this week. You can use one of the prompt questions to get you going. Do the same if your journal has stalled. Make sure at least one entry has a positive mood or outlook.

Try to write at least two or three entries this week, and do it at different times of the day. Think about which time works best for you? When do the words and ideas flow most freely? When do you feel most comfortable and least distracted?

*That was the second session of Journalling School. In the next session we'll look at what to do if you want to restart your journal after a long period of not writing.*

# Session 3: Restarting a journal

*Welcome to the third session of Journalling School. Today's session is about how to restart a journal after you've spent a time not writing.*

When you are in the journalling habit, you tend to gain a momentum that makes it easy to keep going day after day, week after week. But this can sometimes break down.

What happens when you have neglected your journal for a period and want to restart? Perhaps you entered a busy period and your journal fell by the wayside, or perhaps you just lost interest. For whatever reason, you want to make a fresh start.

The thought of cataloguing all that has gone on since you stopped recording your life is likely to be daunting and may put you off starting again. But you might feel that you can't just launch in again as if nothing has happened either. What I suggest is this:

1.  Take a blank sheet of paper – not a page in your journal.

2. Divide the sheet into sections by drawing lines. If it's been just a few months since you stopped, then each space represents a month. If it's been years, each space represents a year.

3. Write the names of the months or the years in each space and then write one or two bullet points of notable events from that month or year. Don't add any detail – just use a word or two or a memory trigger.

4. Tuck the completed sheet in your journal.

Now, start writing in your journal again regularly. If you have to, you can use a new journal, but I'd recommend you use the old one and just start on the next fresh page, because what you're going to be doing is recreating the continuity, repairing the gap.

Once a week (or whenever you feel like it, or have the time), pick one of your months or years and write up the events as you remember them. As you record your memories, cross them off on the sheet. Before long, there will be nothing left on the sheet and you will be back to journaling in the normal way.

You should also treat restarting your journal as an opportunity. Think about why you stopped. Was it because of an aspect of the way you were journalling? Is this a good time to try doing things differently?

# Homework

If you have fallen out of the habit of writing a journal, then try the exercise above. Remember what you were hoping to achieve when you originally started your journal. Consider if that is still what you want, or whether you should take this opportunity to journal differently.

If you've yet to start a journal, and last week's prompts didn't inspire you, try the exercise above. Rather than a few months or years, though, you'll be looking at your whole life. Have a space for each decade or each significant period (e.g. University, newly-wed.) Make bullet notes on the sheet and then start your journal, taking one period of your life each entry.

*That was the third session of Journalling School. In the next session we'll take a longer look at positivity.*

# Session 4: Positive journalling

*Welcome to the fourth session of Journalling School. Today we are going to explore positive journalling, and its mood-altering abilities.*

Often, we are advised to face challenges and work through issues by writing about how we feel in a journal. That is worthwhile, because once you've cleared the air and got those feelings down on paper, I find that they stop eating away at you. It can be as though you have pulled them from your mind and trapped them on the paper, and that's a great result.

However, there comes a time when enough is enough and when what's lacking is a little positivity. Just like you can smile yourself into a good mood, you can write your way into a positive attitude, or confidence, or relaxation. Simply write about one, some or all of these topics:

1. What am I grateful for?
2. What am I looking forward to?
3. If things go well for me, how will I feel next week/month/year?

4. What nice things do people say about me?

5. Who do I love and why?

6. What are my greatest achievements this year/this decade/in my life?

You will end the writing session smiling and feeling warm and confident, which could be enough to make a big difference to the outcomes of your day.

If you have feelings of depression, fear or discontent, you have to acknowledge them first, though, or your positivity will be largely wasted as suppressed feelings keep intruding on your consciousness. So if you want to use your journal to influence your mood in a more positive direction, there are three steps to achieving it.

STEP 1: Write about how you actually feel. Pour out the worries, fears, concerns. Share your depression with the page. Acknowledge what's on your mind.

STEP 2: Keep going as long as you need to. Make sure you write down every aspect of your malaise, even if it covers pages and pages. When you've finished, pause. Let the echoes fade away.

STEP 3: Write down one of the prompts listed above and then answer the question in as much depth as you can.

Followers of Neuro Linguistic Programming (NLP) will recognise this as the Match-Pace-Lead process, but rather than engaging with another person to influence them, you are engaging with yourself. And the influence you create will be very real. When you try this technique you will put down your journal in a different mood from the one in which you picked it up. It is catharsis.

## Homework

One day this week, work through the three steps in a journal entry. Try to do it in one sitting, but spread it over a couple of days if you need to. Make sure you really write it all out, and then give as much space to the positive prompt as you can. Do more than one if you like, and keep the focus positive. Afterwards reflect on how you feel.

*That was the fourth session of Journalling School. In the next session we'll be doing some role playing.*

# Session 5: Role play

*Welcome to the fifth session of Journalling School. Today's session is something of an advanced topic and it won't be for everyone. It is about being someone else for a while.*

This idea is inspired by an exchange in the Arnold Schwarzenegger film "Total Recall" (which started life as a much better short story by Phillip K Dick called "We Can Remember It For You Wholesale".) In the film, our hero, Douglas Quaid, visits the HQ of a company called Rekall Inc. At Rekall, they offer a service which implants false memories of a holiday. Rather than the expense and inconvenience of actually going to a place, you can simply remember the experience.

Doug meets Bob McClane there and explains he wants to have memories of a holiday on Mars implanted. Bob outlines a new optional extra:

`Bob McClane:` What is it that is exactly the same about every single vacation you have ever taken?

`Douglas Quaid:` I give up.

**Bob McClane:** You! You're the same. No matter where you go, there you are. It's always the same old you. Let me suggest that you take a vacation from yourself. I know it sounds wild. It is the latest thing in travel. We call it the Ego Trip.

Doug decides to be a secret agent on his holiday, and the film then gets rather weird. But the point is this: you can use a similar trick in your journal. You can write in the persona of a secret agent, or a visiting alien, or a TV reporter, or whatever your imagination can conceive.

When writing, you can think about what your persona would notice or find interesting, and write about that. One of the most effective roles to play is that of a child, perhaps a younger version of yourself, who doesn't understand much of what is second nature to you. You will find yourself wondering about and questioning all sorts of things you normally take for granted and this can throw up some great insights.

Set yourself the task of staying in this persona in your journal for a few days, perhaps for a week, and just see what emerges. You will undoubtedly write about things that would ordinarily never have made it to your journal, and at the end of the 'Ego Trip' you can evaluate the exercise and decide what you'd like to keep writing about even after you drop the persona.

# Homework

Take an Ego Trip in your journal. Be someone else for a few days. Write about the things that you normally would, but look through different eyes. Focus on what this persona would focus on and write accordingly. Afterwards, go back and read your entries. Think about what emerged that wouldn't normally find its way into your journal. Which of these elements would you like to incorporate in your regular journalling?

If this is just too weird for you, then reverse the situation. Be yourself and write in your normal way, but write about an imaginary day that didn't actually happen. Imagine a dramatic event. If you like, you can include famous people that you don't know. Write just as if this were a normal day. Afterwards, go back and read your account, and think about what is different in the way you wrote this entry. Can some of this find its way into your day-to-day journalling?

*That was the fifth session of Journalling School. In the next session we'll be looking at personal goals and how journalling can help you reach them.*

# Session 6: Personal goals

*Welcome to the sixth session of Journalling School. In today's session we'll be looking at how your journal can help you achieve your personal goals.*

Writing down your personal goals is generally considered to be one of the most important personal development activities you can undertake. But it is only part of the story. Making your goals public, reviewing the goals and progress towards them are important, too and so is planning how you'll achieve them. You can do all of this in your journal.

Firstly, you have to explain what your personal goals are. For each, journal about what the goal is, but also:

- Why this goal is important to you
- What achieving it will mean to you
- When you want to achieve it by
- What plans and ideas you have for achieving it

When I did this myself, I split the goals up and covered one each day for a week, but if the mood takes you, you can do them all in one entry. The idea is to really explore each goal.

Next, you should revisit your goals regularly, perhaps monthly and perhaps one goal at a time. When you do this, write about:

- What you have done to get nearer to the goal(s)
- What you are going to do next
- What other ideas you intend to try
- Whose support you need and how you plan to get it

Note that when you look forward, you don't have to have the answers when you start writing. Next time we'll look at problem solving in your journal, and you'll find when you try the techniques I'll explain then that blank paper is very much your friend.

Here is where your journal and your planner really come together. When you have finished your goal review, transfer all of the ideas and actions into your planner. Where you can, write actions into your calendar on fixed dates. Where you cannot schedule definite actions, schedule planning time or make some entries in your task lists. Also, pop a post it tab or a bookmark in your journal on today's entry so that next month you can review the entry and hold yourself accountable when you review your progress again.

What you'll find when you start to consciously plan and pursue your goals in this way is that they stop being just dreams and start to become conceivable reality that you are working towards. Of all the outcomes you might find journalling gives you, this is perhaps the most tangible and life-changing.

It isn't just your life goals that you can use this technique for. You can use the same approach for any change you want to bring about - say, changing your career or getting fit. Start by writing about the change you want to make, why you want to change and what making the change will mean to you. Then, regularly write about what progress you've made, what you want to try next and what other ideas you have. Use your planner and keep holding yourself accountable.

## Homework

If you have already written your personal goals, then write about them in your journal this week. Pick one or two goals a day and consider them from all angles. In particular, talk about what achieving the goals will mean to you. If you haven't yet written personal goals, then use your entries this week to explore what they might be; think and write about what you want to achieve professionally and personally, at work and in your relationships. Finish the week with a list of 4-8 goals you want to commit to.

Put a note in your planner for when you want to review progress towards your goals. Do it straight away, even if you haven't written your goals yet.

*That was the sixth session of Journalling School. In the next session we'll be looking at problem solving in your journal.*

# Session 7: Problem solving

*Welcome to the seventh session of Journalling School. In today's session we'll be looking at how your journal can help you solve many problems that might beset you.*

Have you ever lain awake at night or woken up early, your mind spinning frantically, fixating on an issue you are facing and refusing you the peace you need to sleep?

If not, have you ever found yourself facing an issue that you can't see how to resolve, that ends up oppressing you, preventing you from enjoying the positive aspects of your life?

Well, your journal can help you with these situations. In previous sessions, we've talked about using your journal to dump such worries, but today we're going to go beyond that. Because actually, journalling can help you not only cope with these problems, but actually resolve them too.

There are ten ways you can use your journal to solve problems.

Actually, there aren't; or if there are, I don't know what they are. But if I wrote that sentence in my journal - "THERE ARE TEN WAYS YOU CAN USE YOUR JOURNAL TO SOLVE PROBLEMS" - I'm sure I could come up with ten.

This is a technique I have used in my own journal to explore thoughts and issues and resolve problems. Here's an actual example I used recently:

> I AM GOING TO LIST TWELVE THINGS I CAN DO WITH THE FAMILY AT THE WEEKEND TO MAKE UP FOR WORKING LATE EVERY DAY THIS WEEK.

And having written that in my journal, I then set about listing my ideas.

Why twelve? Because it was a few more than I thought I'd be able to manage. I did manage twelve, although the last three needed a few minutes of headscratching. If I hadn't had the target number to fulfil, I would have stopped at nine. That would have been a shame, because number eleven was a real gem of an idea.

I have used the technique quite widely already, and giving yourself a stretching target really does pay dividends.

Think about these examples:

- There are ten things I can do right now to save money.

- I can think of five ways to help me stick to the diet I keep breaking.

- Here are twelve things I can do this month to help make my career change.

- There are six ways I can try to repair my relationship with my neighbour.

To reiterate, you don't have to know what any of the numbered things or ways are when you write down that introductory sentence. Writing it down is challenging yourself to fulfil the commitment you just made. Make sure you persist and actually meet the quota, even if some of the ideas seem a bit silly. Often, writing down those silly ideas can be fantastically useful, because it makes you hold them in your head longer than you normally would, where they can inspire other, potentially viable ideas.

## Homework

If you are facing a particular problem, use the technique. Challenge yourself by choosing a number which is more than you think you can come up with. If you believe you might be able to find six or seven ways to earn more money, for instance, write down: *There are ten ways I can start earning more money right away.* Then keep writing until you have listed ten. If you find it easy, then keep going; identify more ideas and next time give yourself more of a challenge.

If you don't have a particular problem, then go back to your goals and apply the approach with one of them. Write something like: *There are six things I can do tomorrow to help achieve my goal to...* As above, don't stop until you've met the challenge, and keep writing of you get there quickly.

Finally, turn your ideas into scheduled activities in your planner, or undated tasks where you can't assign a time and date.

*That was the seventh session of Journalling School. In the next session we'll be looking at keeping things fresh in your journal.*

# Session 8: Keeping things fresh

*Welcome to the eighth session of Journalling School. In today's session we'll be looking at how you can keep things fresh when you get into a journalling rut.*

It is a good idea to introduce new elements into your journalling from time to time, because keeping things fresh makes it easier to maintain your interest and commitment.

So, when things are starting to become a little stale, here is a way to find new inspiration.

Have a look at this web page:

http://blogs.chicagotribune.com/news_columnists_ezor n/2008/01/50-things-ive-l.html

**Chicago Tribune**

## Change of Subject

OBSERVATIONS, REPORTS, TIPS, REFERRALS AND TIRADES

BY ERIC ZORN | E-mail | About | RSS

« Prognosticators give their take on '06 | Main | Audio: Schmich, Williams and I on the smoking ban, e-thanks and other urgent matters in public life »

Thursday, January 03, 2006

## 50 things I've learned in 50 years, a partial list in no particular order

The author lists 50 things he has learned in 50 years. Some of them are humorous, some profound, but every single one of them provokes thoughts and reactions.

I used to have a printout of that article folded and tucked inside my journal. Not every day, but whenever I felt like it, I picked an item - the next in the list - wrote it in my journal and then noted my reactions and explained how my experiences related. This article of fifty points lasted me about three months. Before that one, I worked my way through several similar articles; the web contains thousands of them. Many are themed ('Twenty ways to be a nicer person' or '25 ideas that will make work more enjoyable', for example) and these can provide an interesting focus to your journal for a few weeks.

# Homework

Print off the article linked above, or a similar one. Fold and store it in your journal. At least twice this week, take it out and write about one of the items in the list. First, introduce what you're doing. Then write the item and then react to it. Write down your thoughts - do you agree with the idea or not; have you any relevant experience of having tried something like it before; how would you implement it tomorrow if you had to?

After you've done this a couple of times, decide whether you want to persist with this particular article, or find one that means more to you (Google to find some possible candidates.)

*That was the eighth session of Journalling School. In the next session we'll be looking at some questions that have arisen in comments so far, along with other frequently asked questions about journalling.*

# Session 9: Frequently asked questions

*Welcome to the ninth session of Journalling School. In today's session we'll be looking at some of the questions that have arisen so far and that often come up in relation to journalling.*

So, let's have a time out and look at some questions that have come up. I'll give you my view, but there is scope for argument and you are welcome to add your views in the comments.

## What sort of book or system should I use for my journal?

There's no one answer to this, but it might take some trial and error before you find what is right for you. Here are the characteristics of a journal I'd advocate for someone new to journalling:

1. **Bound.** I advocate a bound book rather than a loose-leaf system, mostly for psychological reasons. When you write on a loose page, you are less likely to take care about what and how you write, because the page can easily be discarded. In a book, though, you will have to live with mistakes and misjudgements, which means you are more likely to take care not to make any. Spiral binding is a bit of a compromise, but I'd always go for a fully case-bound book.

2. **Small but not tiny.** Your journal should be portable. That is not to say it should accompany you everywhere, but when you take vacations, you'll want to take it with you. Even when you go somewhere just for a day, if you know you'll have spare time, you should take the journal with you and write while you're there. I always find the nature of my writing changes with my location, and I like the variety. But your journal should be so small it can fit in a back pocket. I find anything smaller than about A5 discourages proper writing with grammar and structure.

3. **Free format.** I'd strongly recommend you don't buy a dated diary to use as your journal. You might well not write every day and empty pages will taunt you. It is better to just start again after a gap in time without a gap in the book. Pre-dated pages also limit the amount you can write in any one day, whereas I don't believe you should be limited in any way; you should be able to write as much or as little as you want or need to.

4. **Inexpensive.** Once you are firmly in the habit or journalling, you might decide to spend good money on an expensive journal. That's fine. When you're starting, though, it is likely to cause you problems. When you're so worried about sullying those expensive pages, you can end up writing nothing at all. I call this 'journalling stage fright'. Avoid it by using an inexpensive journal, at least for your first volume.

My journal book of choice is the Black n Red A5.

## Can I keep an electronic journal?

Of course you can. Personally, I find this harder than writing by hand. I can't write as quickly as I can type, so my ideas are more fully-formed when I write them by hand. I can always open my book and start writing immediately, whereas it may not be convenient to get a laptop or pad out wherever I am. And I like to see the book filling up gradually. To be able to flick back and forth and to see the odd crossing-out - and remember why I crossed it out - is useful too.

## How much do I have to write?

However much you want or need to. You're not writing lines as a punishment; rather, you are writing as an investment. You are investing time and effort in understanding yourself and the world a little better, in making progress towards your goals, in solving problems, and in building a resource of unimaginable value in the future.

Some days you might want to write and write until your hand aches. Other days you might want to write just a paragraph, or nothing at all. It's all good. There is no minimum word count and there are no deadlines.

## What should I write about?

Hopefully but this stage, you're not short of things to write about, but it is worth thinking about any trends you are finding in your writing and where you want to go in the long term. For example, it is easy to get into the rut of just recording the events of the day without any real comment or reflection. At the other extreme, it can all be about you dumping what's in your head.

I think over the long term everyone needs to find the right balance between being externally focused (what's happened today) and having an internal focus (what am I feeling?) There may be spells in your life when the balance between these has to change. For example, in times of stress it is important to vent your feelings fully because this makes such an enormous contribution to you being able to cope and recover.

Beyond the events of the day and your reactions, though, there is a wealth of things you can write about, as I hope this series has demonstrated. For instance, what are your

44

goals, and how are you working towards achieving them? What are the big news stories currently, and what's your take on them? What would you do if you won the lottery next week or if you were stranded on an isolated island? If you were to throw a dinner party and could invite anyone, who would you like to come and why?

In short, write about whatever occurs to you in the moment, but also invest some time in thinking about what you want to write about in the future. Keep a list of things you want to write about when you have time to write a longer entry.

## How careful should I be in case people read it?

This is a difficult question. There are some benefits you can derive from journalling only if you are totally honest and free to write whatever you feel. There are people who can do that, but I'm not one of them. I have an internal censor that requires me to be as honest as possible, but circumscribe where fragile people and situations are concerned. That means I might sometimes not share all of my feelings with the page.

It's difficult to say why this is; my journal is not written for publication, not for reading by anyone but me. Even my wife doesn't read it, although she's seen me writing in it, often at length. But somehow I feel that if she (or someone else close to me) did ask to read it, I wouldn't want to feel awkward about letting them.

This is a question you'll have to answer for yourself. Do you mind saying 'no' when people ask to read your journal? Is there a risk that people will read your journal without your permission? Do you even worry about what other people think?

## Homework

There's no homework this week, except to consider whether you have any questions that haven't been covered. If you do, reach out online.

> *That was the ninth session of Journalling School. In the next session we'll be looking at the effect of tenses - past, present and future - and how to reflect these in your journalling.*

# Session 10: Past, present and future

*Welcome to the tenth session of Journalling School. In today's session we'll be looking at the effect of tenses - past, present and future - and how to reflect these in your journalling.*

Generally, we write in our journal about the day we are experiencing now. Although we probably write in the past tense ("I visit<u>ed</u> Susan") it is present day we're talking about. But this is a convention, not a rule. There is no reason why we can't journal about the more remote past, or about the future.

In earlier sessions of Journalling School, I have encouraged you to look both backwards and forwards in time in your writing - backwards when you are catching up on a break in journalling, forwards when you are addressing your goals.

Today, we are going to take things a step further and write some time narratives to support change. A time narrative is a story really, but most stories begin and end in the past. These are stories that extend from the past into the future. The crucial difference here is that the ending has yet to be fixed.

Here is a very simple time narrative:

- **In the past** I have wasted money without thinking.
- **Right now** I am starting to record and review my spending and make economies where I can.
- **In the future** I will have built up savings and be financially secure.

Note that this narrative describes a change. The past and the future are very different from each other, and that difference is anchored in the present. The action I am taking now is the catalyst for change.

Here is another example:

- **In the past** I allowed my friends to take advantage of me.
- **Right now** I have decided to stand up for myself, to use assertiveness techniques and say 'no' sometimes.
- **In the future** I will enjoy more balanced relationships where my friends support me too.

I would call these examples 'outline' time narratives, because they summarise the story without giving any detail. Having written your outline, you need to go back and write about each of the three time episodes - the past, the present and the future - and build a much clearer, more detailed picture for each. You might spread this over several days, or decide to settle down for a long entry in your journal in one day.

For your picture of the past, describe how things have been. Give some examples and talk about how these made you feel. Describe why you want to make a change.

For the present, describe what action you are taking or are resolving to take. Keep this is the present tense ("I am saying 'no'" rather than "I will say 'no'".) If you are not sure on what action you need to take, you can use the problem solving techniques we looked at in Session 7. You can also talk to people, read and research in other ways.

For the future, really build a detailed picture of how things will be. Imagine some examples of the new skills or approaches and describe how you will act and how it will make you feel. Spend longer on this that you think is necessary. The time and detail you invest here are key to lasting and effective change. Your unconscious mind will absorb every word and become your invisible ally in helping to bring the change about.

# Tense-shifting

Here is an interesting journaling exercise you can try from time to time. Try to imagine yourself one day in the future, when you'll be recording the events of the day and your feelings. Now write down today what you imagine you would be recording tomorrow.

When you get to tomorrow's session, read back what you wrote and consider how close your predictions came to your actual experience of the day. What had you foreseen perfectly, for instance, and what hadn't you anticipated at all?

Once you've done this a few times, look for themes. Are you surprised regularly by similar factors? Do you have any blindspots? How far do your expectations shape your experiences?

Another spin on this is to write tomorrow's entry based not on what you **EXPECT** to happen, but on what you **HOPE** might happen.

What you're trying to do in this exercise is again to put your subconscious to work. It will try to find a way to produce the positive outcomes you describe, meaning your day is more likely to be a successful one.

# Homework

If there is a pressing change you feel you need to make, then write your own time narrative to describe your journey from the past, through the present and into the future. Start with an outline that resembles the examples above. Then look at each stage in more detail - I'd recommend that you tackle the past on one day and the present and future on subsequent days. Take time out to do any talking or research that you need when it comes to the present.

If you don't have a particular change you need to make, then in your journal write tomorrow's entry today. Describe what you hope will happen as if it already has. Again, use detail to make the picture as vivid as possible and engage your unconscious in making it happen.

*That was the tenth session of Journalling School. In the next session we'll be examining the power of looking back in your journal.*

# Session 11: Looking back

*Welcome to the eleventh session of Journalling School. In today's session we'll be talking about the concept of looking back at earlier journal entries and how this can influence your journalling today.*

I often take the opportunity to look back in my journal. I find it fascinating to read my words of - say - five years ago. Seeing a particular phrase, or even a flourish at the end of a word can spark off a Proust-like reverie in which I am transported to the time of writing. Suddenly, forgotten sights and thoughts are recaptured and for a while I can see the past as vividly as the present day.

Other times I look back to the more recent past. Before I write on the very last page of a book I go back to the front and read the first entry that I would have written two or three months earlier. This can sometimes prompt some thoughts about the main events in the period covered by the book. Now and again I will find there has been a significant change in my life that is only appreciable in hindsight and that without my journal I would never have recognised.

So I encourage you to look back and look often, and to write about what you find. Here are some aspects you might write about:

- What do I know now that I didn't know then?
- What else do I remember about that time?
- How have things changed for me since that time?
- What did I not write about then but perhaps should have?

More than anything, looking back can tell you how far you have come and hint at how much further you might still go. I recommend it highly.

## Homework

Pick a date earlier in your journal - perhaps the first entry you made, or one from an important or difficult time. Read your entry and reflect on the questions listed above. Write about the experience of looking back and the thoughts and feelings it has prompted.

*That was the eleventh session of Journalling School. Next week's session will be an end of term special, reviewing all the sessions so far. After that session,*

*Journalling School will take a break but I'll set you some holiday homework.*

# Session 12: End of term review

*Welcome to the twelfth session of Journalling School. Today's session ends this first term of school.*

Over the past three months or so we have taken a journey together at Journalling School. This is the end of the term and thus a good time to review how far we have come.

We began with why you would want to keep a journal and what benefits there might be in recording your life. We looked at how to get started and how to keep going. We saw how you could restart your journal if the habit has lapsed.

Then we looked over a few weeks about using your journal to effect change. We started with an examination of positive journalling and moved on to using your journal to document and work towards your goals and also to solve problems.

We saw how to keep things fresh in your journal, using exercises and techniques (like the Total Recall ego trip.)

Towards the end of term we paused to think about some common journalling questions like what sort of journal to use and how much to write every day.

There was a session on using time narratives in your journal to write about the past, the present and the future.

Last week we considered the power of looking back in your journal.

And so, we have arrived at the end of the term and with it a break from school, although not (it is to be hoped) from journalling.

I'm setting some holiday homework I think you will enjoy. But keep this book with your journal so you can review it and gain inspiration when you need it.

Image by David Michael Morris, used under Creative Commons Licence

# Homework

Write about what your reasons were for starting a journal. Consider whether you have derived the benefits you expected. Were there any surprises?

Consider which of the exercises you have undertaken has been most enjoyable or most enlightening. Write about why and what you learned.

*Here ends the first term of Journalling School. I hope that the school will return with new ideas, perspectives and exercises after a break. I have some ideas for what to cover next term and would love to hear yours. Please use the comments or email me directly at ray.blake@gmail.com.*

48380542R00035

Made in the USA
San Bernardino, CA
25 April 2017